What is the
BIBLE?

Text copyright © 2003 Sue Graves
Illustrations (except where specified) copyright © 2003 Peter Dennis
This edition copyright © 2003 Lion Publishing

The moral rights of the author and illustrator
have been asserted

Published by
Lion Publishing plc
Mayfield House, 256 Banbury Road,
Oxford OX2 7DH, England
www.lion-publishing.co.uk
ISBN 0 7459 4742 5

First edition 2003
10 9 8 7 6 5 4 3 2 1 0

Acknowledgments
(t – top; b – bottom; c – centre; l – left; r – right)
Cover illustrations: (front) Peter Dennis, Rex Nicholls, Nick Rous,
John Williams; (back) John Williams, Peter Dennis.
Inside illustrations: AKG – London: p. 16b (Erich Lessing)
Bridgeman Art Library: pp. 17t, 21b (Bible Society, London, UK)
The British Library: p. 53t K103314 copyright © The British Library,
Cotton Nero D. IV Reproduced by kind permission of the Trustees
of the Chester Beatty Library, Dublin: p. 17b Corbis UK Ltd:
pp. 10t (Jeffrey L. Rotman), 18t (Raymond Gehman), 19t (Digital
Art), 42t (Paul A. Souders), 53b (Bohemian Nomad Picturemakers),
54l (Jonathan Blair), 54r (Hanan Isachar), 56t (Kelly/Mooney
Photography), 57 (Angelo Hornak), 59bl (Annie Griffiths Belt),
59t (Bettmann) Carolyn Cox: p. 55r Lion Publishing: pp. 20t,
29tr, 38t (David Townsend); 6t/b, 7t/c, 14t, 16t, 20br, 23b, 24, 25tl/tr,
27b, 29tl/c/b, 30r, 35t, 39b, 45c/b, 46b, 56bl, 58b, 60c/b, 61t, 62t/b
(John Williams) Rex Nicholls: pp. 11 (drum), 41t, 42b, 46c, 51, 56bc,
58t Zev Radovan, Jerusalem: pp. 8b, 9b, 22, 32, 33t, 45t Lois Rock:
p. 40 Nick Rous: p. 55l Reproduced by courtesy of the Director
and University Librarian, the John Rylands University Library of
Manchester: p. 15tr Martin Sanders: maps on pp. 21, 27, 31, 37, 49,
55 Trip & Art Directors Photo Library: p. 8t United Nations Photo
Library: p. 58r

Picture research courtesy of Zooid Pictures Limited and Lion
Publishing plc.

Scriptures quoted from the Good News Bible published by The Bible
Societies/HarperCollins Publishers Ltd, UK © American Bible
Society 1966, 1971, 1976, 1992, used with permission.
p. 8 (2 Timothy 3:15), p. 9 (Luke 4:18–19), p. 12 (Luke 1:1, 3),
p. 13 (2 Thessalonians 3:17–18; 2 Timothy 3:16–17), p. 18 (Genesis
9:11–13), p. 20 (Genesis 1:31), p. 22 (Exodus 20:2–5, 7, 8, 12, 13–16,
17 (adapted), p. 25 (Ruth 1:16; 1 Samuel 3:10), p. 27 (Esther 4:16),
p. 28 (Psalm 23: 1–3 [adapted]), p. 29 (Proverbs 11:28; 16:24; 10:5;
Ecclesiastes 11:9; Song of Songs 2:11–13; Psalm 119:105), p. 30
(Amos 5:10–12; Isaiah 9:2, 6), p. 34 (Matthew 1:1), p. 35 (Luke
22:19–20), p. 40 (Matthew 6:9–13; Mark 12:29–31; John 13:34),
p. 46 (Acts 1:1–2), p. 49 (2 Corinthians 13:11–13), p. 51 (Exodus
39:10, 13–14; Revelation 21:14, 19), p. 57 (Luke 11:1–4), p. 58
(John 3:16, Isaiah 2:4; Matthew 18:21–22).

A catalogue record for this book is available
from the British Library

Typeset in Veljovic
Printed and bound in India

What is the
BIBLE?

SUE GRAVES

A LION BOOK

Contents

What is the Bible?

▲ A copy of the Christian Bible can be found in churches and in other Christian places of worship. This one is on a stand called a lectern. People read aloud from the Bible as part of church services.

The Bible is a book – the special book of the Christian faith.

The Christian faith has its roots in the faith of the Jewish people. Both Jews and Christians respect the same ancient writings, which tell them about the God they believe in: the God who made the world and who takes care of it. These writings are the Hebrew Bible, the Bible of the Jewish people. They belong to a time in Jewish history between 2000 and 3000 years ago. Christians call these writings the **Old Testament**.

Christians also believe that God was born into this world as a human being: as a Jew, who knew the special writings of his people. He is known today as Jesus Christ. The second part of the Christian Bible tells about Jesus Christ and his followers — the first Christians. This part of the Bible is called the **New Testament**. It was written in the 100 years after the life of Jesus, nearly 2000 years ago.

WHY READ THE BIBLE?

In the New Testament there are many letters from an older Christian named Paul. He wrote two of them to a young man named Timothy. In one of them Paul explains to Timothy why it is important to read the Bible:

Ever since you were a child, you have known the Holy Scriptures, which are able to give you the wisdom that leads to salvation through faith in Christ Jesus.

▲ The Jewish people read aloud from their special writings when they meet each week in their synagogues. This picture shows the cupboard, called the ark, where the scrolls are kept.

◀ Jesus in the synagogue in Nazareth. It was the custom for all Jewish men to be invited to read from the Bible.

JESUS READS THE BIBLE

In the New Testament there is a story about Jesus reading aloud from the special writings of his people when it was his turn to read in the synagogue in Nazareth. He read these words from the book of the prophet Isaiah:

The Spirit of the Lord is upon me,
because he has chosen me to bring good news...
to set free the oppressed
and announce that the time has come
when the Lord will save his people.

▲ A scroll showing part of the Hebrew Bible in the original language.

What does 'Bible' mean?

The word 'Bible' comes from an ancient Greek word, 'biblia', which means 'books'.

The Christian Bible is a collection of over sixty different books – books of many different kinds, written for different reasons. In them we find the history of the Jewish people and what they knew and understood about God over a period of many years. There are many types of writing in the Bible.

THE HISTORY OF A PEOPLE

In the Old Testament there are many stories about the history of the Jewish people. Sometimes the Jewish people won great battles against their enemies – they believed that God helped them to win. At other times they were defeated. The picture below shows the enemy Assyrian army attacking one of their cities.

TALES BY THE FIRE

Some of the stories in the Bible are stories that had been told from parent to child for generations, such as the stories about how God created the world. Someone wrote them down so they would not be forgotten.

▼ The kind of Old Testament battle shown here is based on an ancient carving.

WARNINGS AND PROMISES

In the Bible are the sayings of people who brought messages from God – prophets. These holy men often dressed in rough brown cloaks and let their hair grow long. Some prophets had visions of the future and of heaven.

▶ Hebrew letters cut into stone.

RULES TO LIVE BY

The Bible tells people God's laws about right and wrong. The great laws were written on tablets of stone.

LETTERS

In the Bible are letters written by some of the first followers of Jesus to teach and encourage one another.

SONGS AND SAYINGS

In the Bible there are songs, or psalms, to God and wise sayings about how to live.

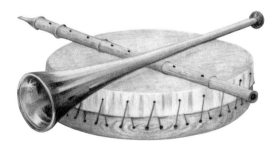

▶ Musical instruments from Bible times.

DID YOU KNOW?

The word 'Bible' is sometimes used for other books: people use the word to hint that a book is the ultimate treasure trove of correct information. So, for example, you might see a 'Gardening Bible' or even a 'Teddy Bear Collector's Bible'. You've probably guessed that they have nothing to do with the Christian Bible!

STORIES OF JESUS

In the New Testament there are books about Jesus, which tell of what he said and did.

Who wrote the Bible?

The books of the Bible were written so long ago, no one really knows who wrote most of them.

Some of the books are not the work of one writer anyway: they are a gathering together of writings. There are collections of stories, laws and hymns, and so on. The unnamed collectors of writings helped make the Bible what it is today.

There are many books in the New Testament which do have named authors. We know who two of them are.

▲ Luke probably used writing materials like these.

LUKE: THE ROAMING REPORTER

A man called Luke, who was probably a doctor, became a follower of Jesus not long after Jesus' lifetime on earth.

He spent time with other Christians and travelled with someone called Paul to spread the message of Jesus in different countries. From what he learned he wrote two books: one about Jesus and the other about what happened to the followers of Jesus. The first is called the Gospel of Luke; the second, the Acts of the Apostles. This is what he says in the introduction to his Gospel:

Dear Theophilus:
Many people have done their best to write a report of the things that have taken place among us. And so... because I have carefully studied all these matters from their beginning, I thought it would be good to write an orderly account for you.

PAUL: A MAN ON A MISSION

Paul, who was a teacher, became a follower of Jesus when he had a miraculous vision. He became a missionary, travelling to different places to tell people about Jesus and his teachings. Paul kept in touch by writing letters. One of the letters in the Bible ends like this:

With my own hand I write this: Greetings from Paul. This is the way I sign every letter; this is how I write. May the grace of our Lord Jesus Christ be with you all.

◀ Paul arranged for his letters to be delivered to the new groups of Christians – the new churches. Here, a messenger delivers a letter to a wealthy Roman woman whose house is big enough for a church meeting.

THE REAL WRITER

Christians believe that the many different people who wrote books of the Bible were all helped in the same way: they were inspired by God.

The great letter writer of the New Testament, Paul, said this:

All Scripture is inspired by God and is useful for teaching the truth, rebuking error, correcting faults, and giving instruction for right living, so that the person who serves God may be fully qualified and equipped to do every kind of good deed.

DID YOU KNOW?

Many of the books of the Bible are named after a person, even though that person may not have written them.

Some of the books of the prophets are named after the prophets themselves, but may have been written by their followers. An example of this is the book of Isaiah.

Other books are named after a person because they are about that person: the book of Jonah is a story about someone called Jonah; so is the book of Daniel.

In the New Testament, some letters are named after the person they are *from*, such as the letter from Jude; others are named after the person they are *to*, such as the letter to Timothy from Paul.

How was the Bible written?

LIBRARY IN A CAVE

In 1947 ancient scrolls were found in caves at Qumran. This is a place by the Dead Sea, in the land of the Bible. Many of the scrolls were parts of the Old Testament. Some of them dated from 400 BCE.

No one knows how the very earliest stories of the Old Testament were first recorded. However, in ancient times the tradition of telling stories was very strong. Parents told children the stories they had heard from their parents... and so on for many generations. Followers of great teachers or prophets also handed on the teaching by retelling it.

It was probably around 3000 years ago, in the time of Israel's great King Solomon, that the first books began to be written. The most usual type of book was the scroll – a long sheet that could be rolled up. The roll was sometimes made of papyrus, which is a bit like paper, or specially prepared leather, called parchment or vellum. People used to write with reed pens. Their ink was made from a mixture of ingredients, often including soot.

Ancient scrolls were kept safe in clay jars.

In New Testament times, scrolls were still used for important writing, but everyday writing was done on sheets of writing material that were folded in half and stitched together down the middle. The little booklet was called a codex. The first Christians often used these everyday booklets to make copies of the stories about Jesus and the letters from people such as Paul that were so special to them.

LAWS TO LAST FOR EVER

The Bible says that God gave Moses ten great laws, known as the Ten Commandments. They were cut into two stone tablets. Like inscriptions on monuments today, this writing in stone was meant to last for ever.

PAPYRUS PAPER

Thousands of years ago in Egypt they had no paper as we know it. Instead they used papyrus – a type of paper that was made from the tall papyrus plants growing in the marshes. Their long, thick stems were stringy inside. These stems could be cut lengthways into thin strips.

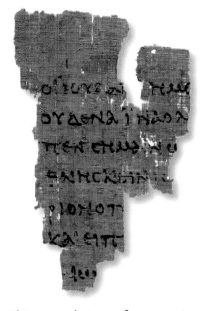

▲ This ragged piece of papyrus is a tiny part of the Gospel of John. It dates from around 100 years after the birth of Jesus. It is the oldest part of the New Testament anywhere in the world.

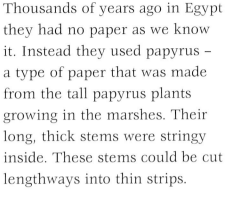

The strips could be lined up in one direction to make a sheet, then more strips placed on top in the other direction.

Then the sheet could be pressed and pounded together to make a strong paper.

DID YOU KNOW?

In Old Testament times people wrote on bits of broken pottery for quick notes and messages. Some writing may also have been done on clay tablets. In the Old Testament God tells the prophet Ezekiel to make a sketch map of the city of Jerusalem on a clay brick.

▶ Here a scribe uses the finished papyrus to write a letter.

Was the Bible written in English?

The Bible started to be written thousands of years ago by people who lived in what we now know as the Middle East. The languages they used for writing and speaking changed over the years, so the Bible is not written in one single language but in three.

◀ Hebrew words from the Bible in schoolboy writing.

HEBREW

Most of the Old Testament was written in Hebrew. When you read a page of English you read across the page from left to right. In Hebrew you have to read from right to left as on the example opposite.

שמע ישראל
יהוה אלהינו
יהוה אחד

▼ The Hebrew letters go from right to left like this:

▼ Here are the Hebrew words with vowels, reading from left to right:

Hear, O Israel,   l'rsy 'ms   sh^{e}ma' yisra'el

the Lord is our God,   wnyhl' hwhy   yahweh 'elohenu

the Lord alone.   dh' hwhy   yahweh 'echad

Hebrew stopped being the language of the Jewish people in the couple of centuries before the time of Jesus and was replaced by Aramaic. However, it was used to create modern Hebrew, which is spoken today by Jewish people in the new state of Israel.

▶ Some Hebrew text from the book of Isaiah from one of the Dead Sea Scrolls, which were found in a cave in Qumran.

ARAMAIC

Part of one of the books of the Bible was written in a language close to Hebrew, called Aramaic. This Aramaic section is in the book of Daniel. It dates from the time when the Persians had an empire including all the lands of the Bible, and was the language of the Persian empire.

Aramaic was spoken for hundreds of years. It was probably the language that Jesus spoke.

▲ A very old copy of Paul's letter to the Romans, probably made around 200 CE. The Greek text is written on papyrus.

GREEK

The New Testament was written in Greek. At that time, nearly all writing was done in Greek and it was understood all through the Roman empire. The New Testament was written in Koine Greek — an everyday form that was easy to use, unlike the official written form with complicated rules. Christians wrote in this kind of Greek because they were ordinary people who probably spoke Aramaic and not Greek in their daily lives.

▲ Although only a small part of the Bible was written in Aramaic, one of the earliest translations was into a form of Aramaic, called Syriac.

DID YOU KNOW?

Jesus is the name of the one Christians follow. It comes from a Hebrew name – the name of a great leader in the Old Testament: Joshua. Jesus would probably have said his own name in the way you would pronounce 'Yehoshua'.

Christians give to Jesus the title 'Christ', a Greek word that means he is God's chosen king. The Hebrew for Christ is 'Messiah'.

THE RAINBOW COVENANT

The book of Genesis in the Old Testament says that God first made a covenant with Noah. It was made after God had kept Noah and the animals safe from a flood in a huge floating box, the Ark. The sign of the covenant was the rainbow.

With these words I make my covenant with you: I promise that never again will all living beings be destroyed by a flood; never again will a flood destroy the earth. As a sign of this everlasting covenant which I am making with you and with all living beings, I am putting my bow in the clouds. It will be the sign of my covenant with the world.

What is the Old Testament?

The first part of the Bible is the Hebrew Bible, the holy book of the Jewish people. Christians call it the **Old Testament**.

The word 'testament' means 'agreement' or 'promise'. Another word that means the same as these is 'covenant', and that is a very important word which is used in the Bible. The Old Testament is so called because it tells of God's agreement with the Jewish people. In particular, the books tell of three great covenants: with Noah, with Abraham and with Moses.

Law books

◀ The books of the Old Testament were written and collected in the thousand years before the time of Jesus. There are different groups of books.

History books

Books of Wisdom

Books of the prophets

THE NIGHT SKY COVENANT

The book of Genesis tells of a covenant with a man called Abraham. God spoke to him and promised to make him the father of a great nation who would bring God's blessing to all the world. He showed Abraham the night sky, and said that Abraham would have more descendants than there were stars in the sky.

▲ The stars at night are too many for anyone to be able to count.

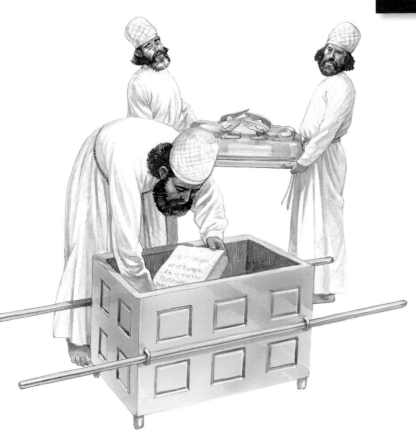

◀ Here the priests put the tablets on which the laws are written into the ark of the covenant.

THE COVENANT IN THE GOLDEN BOX

The book of Exodus in the Old Testament tells of a covenant that God made with a great leader called Moses. The agreement was that the people would live by God's laws: God would be their God; they would be God's people. At the centre of the agreement were the Ten Commandments. These were written on tablets of stone and kept in a golden box – the covenant box, also called the ark of the covenant.

DID YOU KNOW?

Nobody knows what happened to the ark of the covenant. It is likely that is was taken from the temple in Jerusalem when the city was captured by the Babylonians, hundreds of years after the time of Moses.

However the hope that one day the ark might be discovered again is found in many films and stories.

▲ The Bible says: 'God looked at everything he had made, and he was very pleased.'

How does the Bible begin?

The first five books of the Old Testament are known as the Law books, the Torah or the Pentateuch. They are not just full of rules; they are also full of stories – some of the best-known stories in the Bible.

Some stories are set far back in the mists of time and show the relationship between God and the world God made.

GOD'S WORLD

The first story in the Bible is a poem about creation. It tells of God making the world in six days and resting on the seventh. It reminds the listeners that the world is God's and the world was made good.

GOD'S GARDEN PARADISE

The second story in the Bible is the story of God creating a garden paradise in Eden and making a man and a woman – Adam and Eve – to live in it. Sadly, they disobeyed God by eating the fruit from one particular tree in the middle of the garden. In this way, the friendship between God and people was ruined.

▲ The Bible does not say what kind of fruit the forbidden fruit was. Traditionally it is often described as an apple.

Other stories are set in ancient times. They describe the beginnings of the Jewish people. Their great ancestor was a man named Abraham; his son was Isaac, and Isaac's sons were Jacob and Esau.

The nation's story continues with the sons of Jacob. God renamed him Israel, and his twelve sons were the heads of twelve different tribes – the twelve tribes of Israel. One of these sons was Joseph, who was famous for becoming an important official in Egypt and then saving his family from a famine.

▼ The story of Abraham is set in the real world of the Bronze Age, in the lands between the Mediterranean Sea and the Persian Gulf. The arrows show Abraham's travels. He believed that God had promised him the land of Canaan as a homeland.

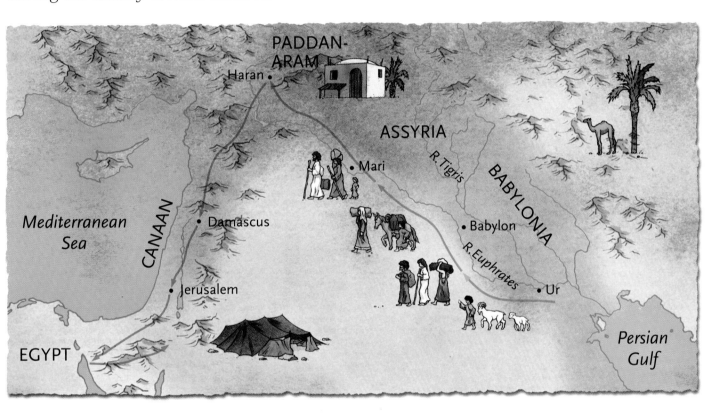

The story of Moses begins at a time when the descendants of Israel were slaves in Egypt. According to the Bible, God helped Moses to lead them to freedom, and back towards the land of Canaan that God had promised to Abraham's descendants. Moses also brought the people laws from God.

▶ This ancient Egyptian painting shows slaves making bricks, as the Israelites had to before Moses led them to freedom.

THE HOLY MOUNTAIN

The story of Moses says that he went to the top of Mount Sinai, between Egypt and Canaan, where, amid thunder and lightning, God gave him the Ten Commandments. These were at the heart of the agreement between God and the Jewish people.

Are there laws in the Law books?

The Law books do contain many laws. The Jewish people say there are 613 altogether. They tell people the right way to worship God and the right way to treat one another.

There are ten great laws, the **Ten Commandments**, which sum up the laws.

THE TEN COMMANDMENTS

1. I am the Lord your God who brought you out of Egypt, where you were slaves. Worship no god but me.

2. Do not make for yourselves images of anything in heaven or on earth or in the water under the earth. Do not bow down to any idol or worship it.

3. Do not use my name for evil purposes.

4. Observe the Sabbath and keep it holy.

5. Respect your father and your mother.

6. Do not commit murder.

7. Do not commit adultery.

8. Do not steal.

9. Do not accuse anyone falsely.

10. Do not desire what belongs to another.

A TENT FOR GOD

In the time when God gave Moses the Law, the people of Israel were nomads living in tents: they had escaped from Egypt but were not ready to claim the land of Canaan for their home. Instead, they travelled through the wilderness. God told Moses to have them make a special tent of worship – the tabernacle. They put this in the centre of their camp.

▲ The tent for the tabernacle was made following God's precise instructions.

KEEPING THE LAW IN MIND

The laws of the Bible told the people of Israel to bind the laws to their heads and arms – to let the laws direct what they thought and what they did. To this day some Jews actually tie tiny copies of the Law to their heads and arms.

▶ This picture shows a leather band with a tiny pocket into which can be put tiny and tightly rolled scrolls with words from the Law written on them. These bands are called phylacteries. In the time of Jesus, phylacteries were made like the ones shown here.

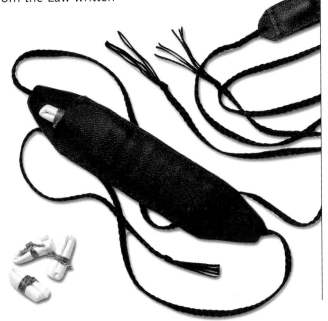

DID YOU KNOW?

Jesus believed that people should not try to look religious so that they would be admired. He criticized some of the religious leaders of his time for showing off by wearing huge phylacteries.

What are the history books?

The twelve history books in the Old Testament tell the history of the Jewish people from the time of Moses onwards.

They begin with the book of **Joshua**. Joshua was the name of the leader after Moses. He led the people into the land of Canaan and helped them settle there. The book of **Judges** describes a time after that when the Jewish people lived as scattered tribes in Canaan. They were often attacked by enemies, but they believed God chose great heroes – called judges – to save them.

The books of **Samuel** tell of the last of the judges, a man named Samuel. God made Samuel a wise judge, and he was greatly respected as someone who could settle quarrels and tell people how to live as God wanted.

When Samuel grew old, the people began to worry about who would be the next leader. They asked for a king. The end of the first book of Samuel and all of the second book are about the first great kings: Saul and David. They beat their enemies and their land was wealthy and at peace. The story continues in the first book of **Kings**.

JOSHUA'S WAR TRUMPET

When Joshua led the people into Canaan, he first had to capture the city of Jericho. God told Joshua what to do. The Israelite army marched silently around the city walls, carrying the ark of the covenant in front of them. Seven priests led them, blowing their trumpets. They marched for six days. On the seventh day, Joshua told them to march as before, but on the seventh time around everyone was to shout as the priests blew their trumpets. The city walls crumbled, and the Israelites took the city.

▲ The kind of trumpet that the priests blew as they marched round Jericho was probably like this. It's called a shofar and is made from a ram's horn.

THE BOOK OF RUTH

The book of **Ruth** tells a story set in the time of the judges. Ruth is a foreign woman, married to an Israelite. When he dies, Ruth stays loyal to her mother-in-law and returns with her to her home in Bethlehem. This is what Ruth promises:

'Your people will be my people, and your God will be my God.'

There, while gleaning grain in the fields, Ruth meets a kind man who marries her and saves the two women from poverty. The story says Ruth was the great-grandmother of David.

DAVID AND THE CITY

After many years of fighting, David became king over all Israel after Saul. He decided to capture a Canaanite fort to make it his new capital. He and his soldiers managed to get in through a water tunnel and conquer the city. He called the city the City of David. It was also known as Jerusalem.

▲ As a boy, Samuel was a helper at a holy shrine. One of his jobs was to keep the lamps burning.

GOD CALLS SAMUEL

God spoke to Samuel when he was just a boy. He heard a voice in the night, when he was sleeping in the holy shrine.

When Samuel knew that the voice in the night was God's, he said:

'Speak; your servant is listening.'

▼ David encourages his soldiers to take a secret route into a strong fort.

What happens next in the history books?

The two books of **Kings** tell what happened after the time of David. He was succeeded by one of his sons, Solomon, who was famous for his wisdom.

After Solomon's death there were quarrels, and the people were divided into two kingdoms. In the northern kingdom of Israel the kings had little respect for God. The kingdom was eventually destroyed by the Assyrians.

Judah, the southern kingdom, survived for a couple of hundred years longer. Then it was defeated by the Babylonians. The people were taken to live in other parts of the Babylonian empire. The city of Jerusalem

▶ The first book of Kings describes how Solomon built the first temple in Jerusalem. Inside, it was covered with gold.

26

was destroyed, as was Solomon's temple. The ark of the covenant was never seen again.

The books called **Chronicles** tell the same story as Kings but they are written in a different way.

Later the Persians took control of the old Babylonian empire. The people of Judah, now called the Jews, were allowed home. The book of **Nehemiah** tells of a man by that name who took charge of rebuilding Jerusalem. A priest named Ezra took charge of the new temple, and that story is told in the book of **Ezra**.

DID YOU KNOW?

Esther is the only book of the Bible that does not mention the name of God.

▲ When the kingdoms split, Jerusalem was still the capital of Judah, but Shechem became the capital of Israel in the north.

THE TWO KINGDOMS

The books of Kings and Chronicles tell of two kingdoms; Israel in the north and Judah in the south.

One of the most famous kings of Israel was a cruel man called Ahab who did not respect God. He had many quarrels with a prophet named Elijah, who proved over and over again that God was stronger and wanted kings to be honest and fair.

One famous king of Judah was Josiah, who became king when he was eight. One day he found a very old book containing God's laws. Josiah called all the people to the temple in Jerusalem to hear the Law being read aloud. The people made new promises to obey God.

THE BOOK OF ESTHER

This book is a story set in the Persian empire. Esther is a beautiful Jewish woman who becomes queen to the emperor. She hears of a plot against the Jews and cleverly uses her charms to persuade the emperor to prevent it from happening. In doing so, she puts herself at risk, but knows she must act to save her people. She says:

'If I must die for doing it, I will die.'

▲ The Jews still celebrate the escape from their enemies at the yearly festival called Purim. One traditional food is biscuits filled with figs.

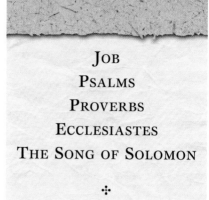

JOB
PSALMS
PROVERBS
ECCLESIASTES
THE SONG OF SOLOMON

✢

THE SHEPHERD PSALM
PSALM 23

This famous psalm gives hope and comfort. Many people think it was written by King David, who began life as a shepherd boy. It begins like this:

The Lord is my shepherd.
I have everything I need.
He lets me rest in green grass
and leads me to fresh water.
He gives me new strength.

▶ David practises playing a simple harp while he watches the sheep grazing in the pasture.

What are the books of Wisdom?

The five so-called books of Wisdom in the Old Testament are all different.

The book of **Job** is a drama about a good man who suffers all kinds of horrible things, and what God thinks and does about that.

The book of **Psalms** was the Israelites' hymnbook. The prayers, songs and poems are still used by Jews and Christians when they gather for worship.

The book of **Proverbs** is full of wise sayings to help people lead good lives.

The book of **Ecclesiastes** asks all kinds of questions about what life is all about. Is it worth anything or does it all come to nothing?

The last book, **The Song of Solomon**, is a collection of love poems.

WISE PROVERBS

Here are some words of wisdom
from Proverbs:

*Those who depend on their wealth
will fall like the leaves of autumn,
but the righteous will prosper like the
leaves of summer.*

*Kind words are like honey –
sweet to the taste and good for
your health.*

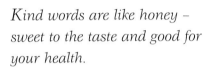

*A sensible person
gathers the crops
when they are
ready; it is a disgrace
to sleep through the
time of harvest.*

WARNING TO THE YOUNG

Here is advice for the young from
Ecclesiastes:

*Young people, enjoy your youth. Be happy
while you are still young. Do what you want
to do, and follow your heart's desire. But
remember that God is going to judge
you for whatever you do.*

THE SONG OF SOLOMON

In spring the hills of the
Bible lands are bright with
flowers – a sight that inspired
the writer of the Song of
Solomon.

*The winter is over;
the rains have stopped;
in the countryside the flowers
     are in bloom.
This is the time for singing;
the song of doves is heard
     in the fields.*

DID YOU KNOW?

Psalm 119 is the longest
psalm in the Bible. It is
in 22 sections – each one
matching a different letter
of the Hebrew alphabet. It
praises God's Law. Here is
one famous line:

*Your word is a lamp to guide
me and a light for my path.*

ISAIAH
JEREMIAH
LAMENTATIONS
EZEKIEL
DANIEL
HOSEA
JOEL
AMOS
OBADIAH
JONAH
MICAH
NAHUM
HABAKKUK
ZEPHANIAH
HAGGAI
ZECHARIAH
MALACHI

❖

The five longest books of the prophets, Isaiah, Jeremiah, Lamentations, Ezekiel and Daniel, are called the 'major prophets'. The shorter books are called the 'minor prophets'.

Who were the prophets?

Prophets are people who speak God's message to others.

The Old Testament prophets were quite a mixed lot! For example, Isaiah belonged to the royal family, while Amos and Micah were farmers. All of them claimed to bring people words from God.

Many of the books of the prophets are written as if the prophet was actually speaking. In fact, the writings were probably put together by the followers of the prophets.

WARNING THE WICKED

Sometimes the prophets warned people about their wicked ways. They said that God would put an end to their wickedness.

Here is what Amos said to the rich people of Israel:

You people hate anyone who challenges injustice and speaks the whole truth in court. You have oppressed the poor and robbed them of their grain. And so you will not live in the fine stone houses you build or drink wine from the beautiful vineyards you plant. I know how terrible your sins are...

GIVING HOPE

When the people of Israel were beaten by their enemies, their kings were killed. The prophets began to speak of a king whom God would send who would change everything. The word for God's chosen king was Messiah. Christians believe that Jesus was the Messiah.

Here is what the prophet Isaiah said:

The people who walked in darkness have seen a great light.
They lived in a land of shadows, but now light is shining on them.
A son is given to us!
And he will be our ruler.
He will be called, 'Wonderful Counsellor',
'Mighty God', 'Eternal Father',
'Prince of Peace'.

1. **Amos** and **Hosea** warned the people in the northern kingdom of Israel to obey God. Hardly anyone listened. The kingdom was defeated in 722 BCE.

2. **Isaiah** and **Micah** warned the people in the southern kingdom of Judah to obey God, or else Assyria would defeat them.

3. Assyria had problems. The story of **Jonah** shows that God was ready to forgive even wicked people, but **Nahum** rejoiced that the Assyrians were defeated by the armies of Babylon in 612 BCE.

4. **Jeremiah** warned that the Babylonians would defeat Judah. **Zephaniah** and **Habakkuk** also gave this warning.

5. The writer of **Lamentations** and **Obadiah** mourned the defeat of Jerusalem in Judah.

6. **Ezekiel**, **Daniel** and the second part of **Isaiah** brought hope to the defeated people of Judah. They had been taken to Babylon, but the prophets said God would bring them home.

7. The people returned to Jerusalem. **Haggai**, **Zechariah** and **Malachi** gave them hope.

Nobody knows for sure where or when the prophet **Joel** spoke his prophecies!

THE PROPHETS IN THEIR TIME

- 3 • Nineveh
- 6
- 4 • Babylon
- 1 • Samaria
- Jerusalem •
- 2 5 7

▲ The numbers on this map show you the places mentioned in connection with the different prophets listed on the left.

GOD'S FORGIVENESS

The story in the book of the prophet Jonah is all about forgiveness. God tells Jonah to warn the Assyrians to change their wicked ways or God will punish them. Jonah runs away, because he hates the Assyrians, and gets on a ship to escape from God. God sends a storm and Jonah asks to be thrown into the sea so the boat's crew will be safe. A huge fish swallows Jonah and takes him to land. Then Jonah goes to warn the Assyrians. They change their ways and, much to Jonah's dismay, God does forgive them!

✛

This is a list of the
Deuterocanonical
books. They are
not all included
in all Bibles.

▶ The people who
copied the Bible by
hand took very
great care not to
make errors
because they
believed that every
word was holy.

Why are some Bibles longer than others?

Some Christian Bibles have a longer Old Testament than others. This is why:

The Jewish scriptures were written over many hundreds of years. Even before all of them were written, the people of Judah began to collect their important writings together. The Jews continued to collect their scriptures when they were in exile and after they returned to Jerusalem. By a couple of hundred years before the time of Jesus, in the time of the Greek empire, there were Jews living in different places all over the empire. Every community wanted to have a collection of scriptures.

The Bible was in Hebrew, but by then more people understood Greek. Seventy scholars set to work to make a translation so each community could have a copy. It is known as the Septuagint – from the Latin word for seventy.

The Septuagint was used by the first Christians and is the basis of the Old Testament in some Bibles, particularly those used by Roman Catholic Christians today.

However, when the Jews finally chose which special writings to include in their Bible, some of the books from the Septuagint were considered not important enough. So the Jews had a shorter collection than the Christians. Then about five hundred years ago, Christians began to question what was in the Bible. Some

Protestant Christians decided the shorter collection was better. The extra books are sometimes called the Deuterocanonical books, or the Apocrypha.

JUDAS MACCABEUS

One of the best-known stories in the longer Old Testament is about Judas Maccabeus. He lived in a time when the Greeks had conquered the land of the Jews. They had even put statues of Greek gods in the Jewish temple. Judas and his brothers led a rebellion to clean out the temple. Then they rededicated it to God.

▼ Judas Maccabeus leads a joyful procession of priests and people into the temple in Jerusalem.

▲ Jewish children celebrate the story of Judas Maccabeus.

DID YOU KNOW?

The story of Judas Maccabeus is at the heart of the Jewish festival of Hanukkah. Part of the celebrations include lighting a candle or a lamp every day for the eight days of the festival – remembering the eight days when Judas Maccabeus rededicated the temple.

When the writers of the books of the New Testament were writing about Jesus and his life, they did not think of it as a new story which was completely separate from the stories of their ancestors in the Old Testament. They showed clearly how Jesus was descended from the most famous king, David. They also believed that he was the special leader, or king, spoken about by various prophets.

This is how Matthew starts his story about Jesus:

This is the list of the ancestors of Jesus Christ, a descendant of David, who was a descendant of Abraham.

What is the New Testament?

The New Testament is the second part of the Christian Bible. The Old Testament, Christians believe, tells of God's first agreement with people. They believe that Jesus was God's special king, God's Son, come to make a new agreement, or covenant, with people.

There are three different types of book in the New Testament.

History Books

◀ These are the four Gospels that tell the story of Jesus' life, death and resurrection, and the Acts of the Apostles, which tells what happened to his followers afterwards and how the news about Jesus spread through the world.

Letters

◀ ▲ These were written by a man called Paul and others either to groups of new Christians in different places or to individuals. They gave advice or encouragement.

Revelation

◀ The vision of a man named John of a new heaven and a new earth. It is a difficult book to understand and some people believe that it is written in a sort of code.

THE NEW COVENANT

The New Testament is so called by Christians because they believe it tells of the new agreement that Jesus talked about.

The promise was made when Jesus shared a last meal with his disciples. This is what Luke says:

Then he took a piece of bread, gave thanks to God, broke it, and gave it to (his disciples) saying, 'This is my body, which is given for you. Do this in memory of me.' In the same way, he gave them the cup after the supper, saying, 'This cup is God's new covenant sealed with my blood, which is poured out for you.'

▲ Since the time of Jesus his followers have shared bread and wine together as he said. When they do so, they remember the agreement, believing that those who follow Jesus are welcomed into God's everlasting kingdom.

A COVENANT FOR ALL

Jesus' followers travelled around telling everyone about Jesus' life and the new covenant made with God through him. They wanted the news to spread to everyone – not just Jews.

▼ Here, Peter, one of Jesus' disciples, is visiting the house of a Roman man named Cornelius to tell him about Jesus.

35

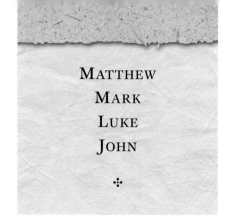

MATTHEW
MARK
LUKE
JOHN

✣

GOSPEL TRUTH

Sometimes people finish what they are saying with the words 'and that's the Gospel truth'. It means they are claiming that what they are saying is as true as Christians believe the Gospels to be.

What are the Gospels?

Four of the history books of the New Testament are about Jesus. They are called the Gospels: the Gospels of **Matthew**, **Mark**, **Luke** and **John**.

Matthew, Mark and Luke say lots of the same things. John's Gospel is quite different from the other three. However, all four Gospels are very clear about one thing: Jesus preached a message of love – love for God and love for other people. He taught in his home region near the inland sea of Galilee and in the big city of Jerusalem.

He was accused by his own people of being a troublemaker. They came and arrested him when he was visiting Jerusalem. They had the Roman rulers execute him: he was nailed to a cross of wood, crucified.

THREE GOSPELS TOGETHER

The Gospels of Mark, Matthew and Luke have a lot in common.

Scholars think that the Gospel of Mark was written first and that Matthew and Luke read Mark and used it in their own writing.

They probably had another source of information which they both used, but no one has a copy of it today. Scholars sometimes call this source of information Q (from the German word Quelle, meaning source).

Matthew and Luke also did some finding out of their own, and have bits that are special to their Gospel. Matthew, Mark and Luke's Gospels are often called the Synoptic Gospels.

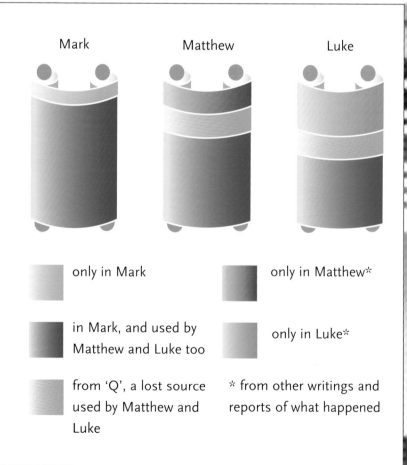

only in Mark

only in Matthew*

in Mark, and used by Matthew and Luke too

only in Luke*

from 'Q', a lost source used by Matthew and Luke

* from other writings and reports of what happened

Jesus was laid in a tomb by his friends. Three days later, they began to see him again. They believed he was alive.

Forty days later, Jesus went away, 'to heaven'. Shortly after that, God gave Jesus' followers the courage and wisdom they needed to spread the message of Jesus... his message of love and the promise that death was not the end.

DID YOU KNOW?

Although the Gospels are the first books in the New Testament they were probably not the first to be written. Some of Paul's letters are probably the earliest part of the New Testament.

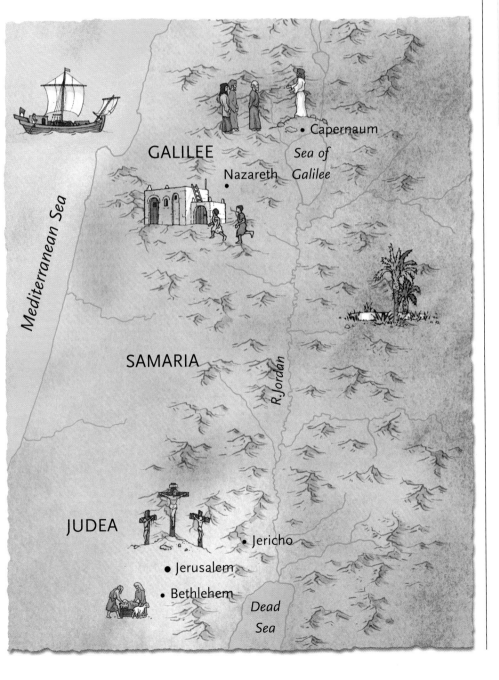

◀ This map shows places that the Gospels talk about. Jesus was born in Bethlehem and grew up in Nazareth. He became a preacher and moved to Capernaum, but travelled all around the country, especially Galilee. It was in the capital city of Jerusalem that he was arrested and condemned to death.

Where is the Christmas story found?

The stories of Jesus' birth are two of the best known in the Bible. They are found in the Gospels of Matthew and Luke. The stories are quite different from one another, but Christians today often put the stories together to make a single story, beginning with Luke.

▲ Sheep still graze on the hills near Bethlehem.

▼ Shepherds come to see the baby in the manger.

THE ANGELS AND SHEPHERDS

The Gospel of Luke tells the story of an angel coming to visit a young woman named Mary in a town called Nazareth. The angel told her that she was going to have a son: God's Son. Not long after, Mary and her husband-to-be, Joseph, travelled to Joseph's home town of Bethlehem. It was famous as the birthplace of the people's great King David of long ago. In the crowded town, Mary and Joseph sheltered in an animal room, and there Jesus was born. Mary used an animal manger as a cradle.

Angels appeared to shepherds on the hillside, and told them to go to see the baby – God's own king.

Later, Mary and Joseph went to the temple to give thanks for the baby, and two people there recognized that Jesus was very special.

Then the family went back to Nazareth.

THE WISE MEN

Matthew's story sets out the long family history of Joseph, going back to the time of King David and Abraham. It says that Mary was pregnant before she married Joseph, but an angel told Joseph to look after her and the baby.

Jesus was born in Bethlehem. Wise men came from far away in the East to find a new king. First they visited King Herod in Jerusalem. When Herod found out that God's promised Messiah was to be born in Bethlehem, he sent the visitors there. The wise men brought Jesus gifts: gold, frankincense and myrrh.

Then an angel warned the wise men not to tell Herod about the baby, so they went home another way. An angel told Joseph to escape with his family to Egypt. Jesus was safe when Herod's soldiers came to try to kill him. A few years later, Joseph heard that Herod was dead. Then he took his family back to Nazareth.

▶These children are taking part in a traditional nativity play.

DID YOU KNOW?

The stories about the beginning of Jesus' life were probably not known to the people he grew up with.

The Gospels tell us that the people in Jesus' home town of Nazareth had no idea that the young Jesus was special.

It was the first Christians, who believed that Jesus rose from the dead, who saw how special he was, and they wanted to write an account of his life from the very beginning.

NATIVITY PLAYS

Every year, all around the world, the two Bible stories of Jesus' birth are retold at Christmas. Another word for birth is 'nativity', so the Christmas story is often called the nativity story. When the story is acted it is a nativity play.

▲ Jesus often went to the hills to be alone with God and to pray.

What do we know about Jesus?

The stories of Jesus talk about his work as a preacher and teacher. Crowds gathered to hear him speaking and he would sometimes talk to them for hours, telling stories or explaining important things about how to live. Many sayings of his are recorded.

LORD'S PRAYER

One day Jesus' friends asked him to help them learn how to pray. The prayer he taught them is still used by Christians all over the world. Both Luke and Matthew record this prayer:

Our Father in heaven:
May your holy name be
  honoured;
may your Kingdom come;
may your will be done on
earth as it is in heaven.
Give us today the food
  we need.
Forgive us the wrongs we have
done, as we forgive the wrongs
that others have done to us.
Do not bring us to hard testing,
but keep us safe from the Evil
One.

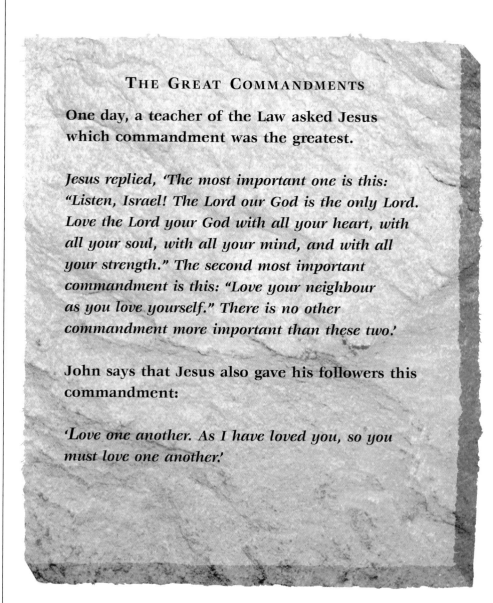

THE GREAT COMMANDMENTS

One day, a teacher of the Law asked Jesus which commandment was the greatest.

Jesus replied, 'The most important one is this: "Listen, Israel! The Lord our God is the only Lord. Love the Lord your God with all your heart, with all your soul, with all your mind, and with all your strength." The second most important commandment is this: "Love your neighbour as you love yourself." There is no other commandment more important than these two.'

John says that Jesus also gave his followers this commandment:

'Love one another. As I have loved you, so you must love one another.'

MIRACLES

The Gospel writers say that Jesus gave many signs, or miracles, which showed what a special person he was. There were different kinds of miracles. Here are some of them:

In one story, told in all four Gospels, a huge crowd gathered to listen to Jesus. As it grew late, Jesus wanted to give the people something to eat. A young boy had five loaves and two fish. Jesus blessed the food, and it was enough for everyone. There was even some left over!

DID YOU KNOW?

People often wanted to see miracles, but Jesus clearly did not want to be known for that sort of thing alone. He was eager to teach them about God and about how to live as God wanted. He welcomed everyone to live as God's friends – as part of what he called 'the kingdom of God'.

Jesus healed many sick people with just a touch: blind people could see, lame people could walk. He even raised people from the dead, such as the daughter of a man named Jairus who came to ask Jesus for help.

One time, Jesus and his disciples were in danger when they were out in a boat on Lake Galilee. A storm blew up and Jesus told the wind to be quiet. Immediately the storm came to an end.

What are the parables?

Jesus often told stories to the crowds who gathered. These stories are called parables. Jesus gave his listeners clues about these stories: 'If you have ears to hear, listen to the message.'

Here are some of the stories:

▼ Jesus often uses the image of a shepherd and his sheep to describe the way God looks after people.

THE PARABLE OF THE LOST SHEEP

There was a shepherd who had a 100 sheep in his care. One night as he was counting them, he noticed that one of them was missing. The shepherd left the other ninety-nine sheep and set off into the night to look for the lost sheep. When he found the sheep, he picked it up and carried it safely home. The shepherd was so happy that he held a party for all his neighbours in the village.

Jesus explained that the lost sheep is like a sinner who is sorry for what they have done wrong and turns back to God.

▼ The Jewish people considered pigs to be unclean. The lost son in Jesus' parable had the worst job imaginable – looking after pigs.

THE PARABLE OF THE LOST SON

There was once a father who had two sons. They were going to inherit everything from him when he died. The younger son did not want to wait. His father sadly agreed to give him his share early, and the younger son left home to live far away. He had a great time until his money ran out. Then he was so hungry he had to get a job looking after pigs.

He decided to go home to his father and say that he was sorry. His father was looking out for him and held a great party to welcome his son home.

Jesus wanted to show people that God is like that father, always waiting and hoping that people will come back to him.

THE GOOD SAMARITAN

One day, a teacher of the Law asked Jesus to explain what it meant
to 'love your neighbour'. In the story known as the Good Samaritan,
Jesus gives his answer. A man begins a journey from Jerusalem to
Jericho. On the lonely road, he is mugged and left for dead. A priest
from the temple comes along, but hurries by. A helper from the
temple comes along. He takes a look but hurries on without
helping. Then comes a Samaritan – someone from a different
region, an outsider. He stops and helps the man. He takes him to
an inn, looks after him and pays for extra care.

'Who was neighbour to the man?' asks Jesus.

The answer is clear: 'The one who was kind to him.'

DID YOU KNOW?

Jesus told his disciples that
there was a reason for telling
parables. To some, the story
was just a story; to others,
the parables helped them
understand more about God
and how to live in God's
kingdom. Those people saw
the deeper meaning.

The week before Easter is the most important week of the year for Christians. It is called Holy Week. It starts on Palm Sunday when they remember how Jesus went into Jerusalem to a great welcome from the palm-waving crowds.

▼ Jesus breaks the bread to share it with his disciples at their last supper together. Here Judas, one of the disciples, is leaving to betray Jesus.

Why is the crucifixion important?

The writers of the Gospels in the New Testament talked mainly about the last part of Jesus' life. This shows that they believed that the last part of his life and the way he died was very important. What was even more important was that they believed that Jesus' death was not the end but that he came back to life afterwards – he was resurrected – and appeared to many people before going to heaven.

On the Thursday after Palm Sunday Jesus had his last supper with his disciples. He knew that one of them would betray him to the religious leaders. They believed he was a troublemaker and later sent soldiers to arrest him. He was taken away for an unfair trial.

◀ This pavement is part of the 'way of the cross', or Via Dolorosa. This is the route which Jesus would probably have walked to the place where he was crucified. It can still be seen in Jerusalem today.

On Friday Jesus was taken to the Roman governor who was in charge of Jerusalem at the time. He condemned him to death, so he was whipped and led out to be crucified. He had to walk through the city carrying a part of his cross before coming to the place where he was crucified, along with two criminals.

Christians believe that through Jesus' death they get forgiven for all the bad things they do and become friends with God again. Jesus loved them so much that he was willing to die for them although he had done nothing wrong himself.

On Sunday some of Jesus' friends came to the tomb where his body had been placed. When they got there the tomb was empty and later Jesus appeared to them. He was alive again!

Christians believe that Jesus' resurrection proves that there is life after death, and gives hope even in the darkest times when people they love die.

EASTER GARDEN

The story of Jesus' death and resurrection is the story that Christians remember at Easter. The day of the crucifixion is called Good Friday and the day of the resurrection Easter Sunday. One tradition is to create a tiny Easter garden showing the crosses on a hillside and the empty tomb.

▶ The cross is the most well-known symbol of the Christian faith. It is frequently used to adorn churches and Christian homes.

▼ A doctor named Luke wrote one of the Gospels. He also wrote the Acts of the Apostles. It begins with the words shown here.

Dear Theophilus:
In my first book I wrote about all the things that Jesus did and taught from the time he began his work until the day he was taken up to heaven. Before he was taken up, he gave instructions by the power of the Holy Spirit to the men he had chosen as his apostles.

▼ Stephen was put to death by stoning. This meant that people kept throwing stones or rocks at him until he died.

What happened after Jesus?

The fifth history book of the New Testament is called the **Acts of the Apostles**. The word apostle means 'one who is sent', and was the name given to the special band of followers Jesus called together. The book of Acts tells us what they did after Jesus went to heaven.

PETER SPEAKS TO THE CROWDS

Acts begins with the story of the apostles believing they have been given strength from God to tell the news about Jesus. One called Peter immediately started speaking to the crowds in Jerusalem.

▼ Jerusalem in the time of Peter.

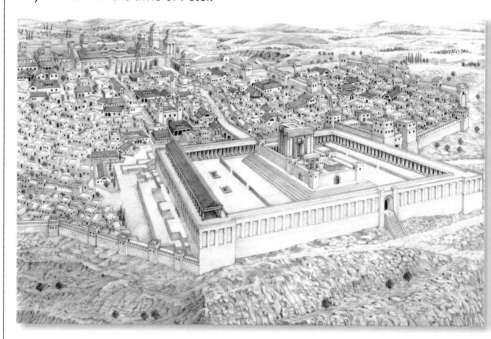

STEPHEN IS MARTYRED

The religious leaders became very angry when they saw people becoming followers of Jesus. One of the new Christians, Stephen, was stoned to death and a religious teacher named Paul simply watched. Stephen was the first Christian to die for his beliefs. He is the first Christian martyr.

When Paul was converted, he was travelling from Jerusalem to Damascus. He saw a bright light and heard Jesus speaking.

People nowadays sometimes describe a sudden change of mind as a Damascus Road experience – a sudden conversion from one way of thinking to another. They may also say that the new ideas came to them in a flash of light.

▼ The book of Acts talks mainly about what Peter and Paul did. It does not say what happened to many of the other friends of Jesus or to his mother, Mary. However it is likely that women had an important role in the early Christian communities.

PAUL'S CONVERSION

Later, Paul had an unusual experience in which he believed he heard Jesus speaking to him. He was converted to being a Christian, and spent the rest of his life helping spread the news.

How did Christians stay in touch?

The Acts of the Apostles tells of how the news about Jesus spread, and of the work of a man named Paul.

Soon there were groups of Christians in different cities. As Paul and other Christians travelled with the news, they wanted to keep in touch with these groups: the first churches.

Paul wrote a lot of letters, and thirteen are in the Bible. They are named after the people to whom they were sent, for example the letter to the Romans was from Paul to the Christians in Rome; his letter to Timothy was to a friend of his named Timothy.

In the end, Paul was arrested for what he was doing, because Christianity was not allowed in the Roman empire at that stage. He was sent to Rome for trial, where he was kept imprisoned in a house where he lived. He dictated some letters to a scribe from there.

▼ On a few occasions Paul was shipwrecked, but every time he was saved from death.

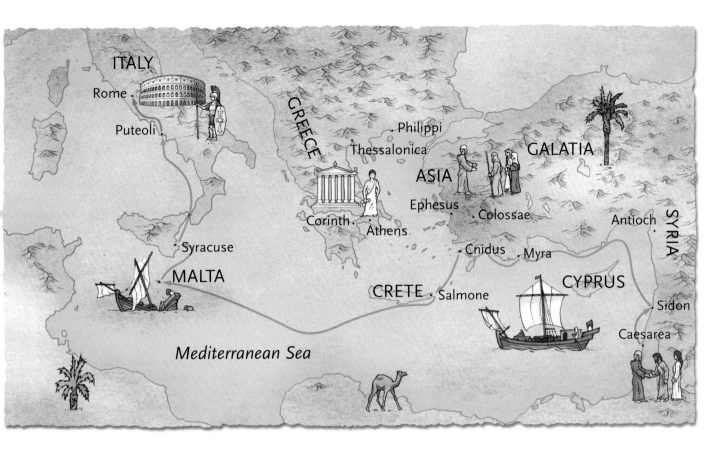

There are other letters in the Bible after those of Paul. They are all written to new Christians, to help them in their faith. In spite of the names of the letters, people no longer know exactly who wrote them or exactly who they were for.

The letters by Paul and others were written for a variety of reasons. They encouraged people in their faith and told them not to give up, even if they were unpopular because of it.

They answered questions about the faith.

They helped settle disagreements between people.

They gave advice to Christians about how to live, and to church leaders. In one of Paul's letters to the church in Corinth he sums up all his advice in the words shown here:

▲ Here is a map showing many of the places which Paul visited on his first two journeys and the route of his last great journey, which ended in Rome.

Strive for perfection; listen to my appeals; agree with one another; live in peace. And the God of love and peace will be with you.

The grace of the Lord Jesus Christ, the love of God, and the fellowship of the Holy Spirit be with you all.

Does the Bible describe heaven?

The last book of the New Testament is the book of **Revelation**. It was written by a man called John. He had to work in the prison camps on the island of Patmos. He was there because he had been caught spreading the news about Jesus.

One day, he writes, an angel spoke to him and gave him amazing visions.

▼ In his description of heaven John talks of it having streets of gold. All the people are dressed in white – a symbol of purity.

He was told to send messages to seven churches —
words of warning and of encouragement in times of
trouble.

Then he saw a vision of heaven... a vision of a great
battle between good and evil, and the final victory of
God and God's goodness. He saw Jesus promising to
come and welcome people to God's wonderful heaven.

The mysterious visions have puzzled Christians for
years! Many believe that the people for whom the book
was written may have understood it more easily...
rather like some kind of code.

To this day, however, the pictures have provided hope
and encouragement for many in times of trouble.

DID YOU KNOW?

Many ideas about what
heaven is like come from
the book of Revelation.
For example, people talk of
pearly gates, saints dressed
in white and a city of gold.

SYMBOLS IN THE BOOK OF REVELATION

In John's description of a new heaven the number
twelve and jewels play an important part. Twelve
stands for the twelve tribes of Israel, and for the
twelve apostles.

In the book of Exodus Moses
received instructions about how to
make garments for the priests. One of
the garments a priest wore was the breast
plate. It is described as follows:

*They mounted four rows of precious stones on
it... These were mounted in gold settings. Each
of the twelve stones had engraved on it the
name of one of the sons of Jacob, in order
to represent the twelve tribes of Israel.*

John says:

*The city's wall was built on twelve foundation stones,
on which were written the names of the twelve
apostles... The foundation stones were adorned
with all kinds of precious stones.*

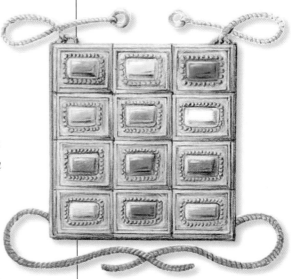

▲ The high priest's breast plate.

Who handed on the stories?

After the time of Jesus, the Christian faith spread to many people. About 150 years after the time of Jesus, the church leaders met to talk about the various writings they had about Jesus. They thought hard about all the documents they had, but decided that some didn't meet the test they had set for what should be in their scriptures. In this way they chose which books would be in the New Testament.

In 312 a Roman emperor named Constantine became a Christian and declared the faith to be the official religion of the empire. At last Christians could meet openly, and the emperor was happy for them to do what was needed to help the faith grow. Some church leaders met in 363 in a town called Laodicea to make a final list of what to include in the Bible. They put the collection of Christian writings together with the longer collection of Jewish writings. A similar meeting happened in 397 in

◄ Chi and Rho are two Greek letters – the first two letters of the word for Christ. Constantine chose the Chi-rho symbol as his emblem.

◄ The night before an important battle Constantine had a vision of a cross and words which said, 'By this sign you will conquer.' He won the battle.

Carthage to sort out the final details. In this way, the official Bible, or canon, of scripture was decided.

Already, Christians in different countries had begun making translations of parts of scripture. In 384, the leader of the church, Pope Damascus, arranged for someone called Jerome to translate the Bible into the language of the Roman empire, Latin. The translation is called the Vulgate. It became the most widely used Bible in all the world.

In the centuries that followed, copies of the Bible were made, but every one had to be made by hand. It was not until the invention of printing in 1450 that it became possible to produce any book quickly. The first book to be printed was a Bible, in Latin, in 1456.

▲ Here is a page from the Lindisfarne Gospels. The words are in Latin.

TRANSLATIONS OF THE BIBLE

In the 15th century there was a huge argument in the church when people began to question if the church leaders were being faithful to the teachings of the Bible. The Protesters, or Protestants, wanted people to read the Bible for themselves. Soon, translations were being made into the main European languages.

Around the same time, people from Europe began exploring parts of the world they had known little or nothing about before. The people they met did not know about Christianity. Missionaries began to travel to other countries to tell about their faith. Soon, the Bible was being translated into many different languages.

By now the Bible has been translated into 2000 languages. There are about 7000 languages in the world.

▼ This translation of the Bible is in Chinese.

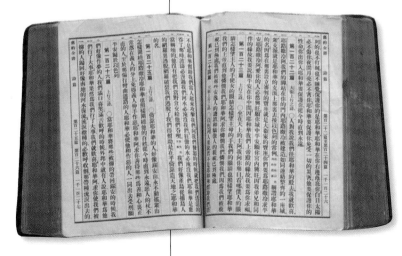

As well as reading the Bible aloud at weekly services parts of the Bible are also read at special services such as baptisms, weddings and funerals.

DID YOU KNOW?

Lent is the season of the Christian year leading up to Easter. It remembers the time when Jesus went into the wilderness alone to think about his new work as a preacher and teacher. Christians often choose Lent as a time to think more about their own faith, and they may well choose to spend more time than usual reading the Bible.

Who reads the Bible?

Christians all value the Bible as the book of their faith. All over the world today, Christians read the Bible.

The Bible is read aloud in many church services.

Many Christians like to have a Bible of their own. Some read it every day. Others only read it occasionally – perhaps at a festival such as Christmas, or when they want to find words of help or wisdom.

GOSPEL PROCESSION

In Catholic, Orthodox and some Anglican churches there is often a special procession before the reading from the Gospel. The Bible may have incense wafted over it, and the priest may kiss it as a sign of its holiness. This is done for the Gospel reading because the Gospels are considered to be the most important part of the Bible. They are very special since they contain the words of Jesus. In these churches it is only the priest who reads the Gospel while other readers will read from the Old Testament and other parts of the New Testament.

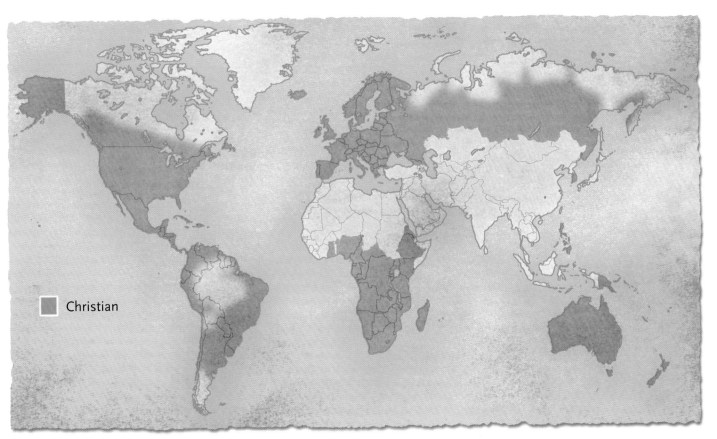

Christian

▲ This map shows the areas where Christianity is an important religion. In recent years many countries have accepted immigrants from other parts of the world and as a result have become multi-faith communities. In fact Christians can be found all over the world.

BIBLE STUDY

Some Christians meet together outside church services to read the Bible and talk about what it says to them. Small groups may meet in someone's house. They will choose a section to read and then discuss what it means to them in their day-to-day life.

▲ Christian families want their children to know the Bible. They often choose a children's Bible to begin with. This will retell some of the best-loved stories, often with bright pictures.

How do you use the Bible?

The Bible contains a lot of words, and if you look inside a real translation of the Bible it can seem quite difficult to know where to begin.

Most modern Bibles are organized in a way that will help!

Look in the front of the Bible for a list of the books. This list will tell you which page to go to.

On the page you will see the name of the book. There will be larger numbers to mark the chapters. Some Bibles will even say 'Chapter 1' and so on.

Within the words you will see tiny numbers. These are the numbers of the verses.

People use the name of the book, the chapter and the verse to help find the part they want.

For example try looking up some of the stories on this page.

▲ Nowadays people can look up parts of the Bible by using their computer.

◀ The story of Noah starts at the book of Genesis, chapter 6, verse 9 and ends at chapter 9, verse 17. (This might be shown as Genesis 6:9 – 9:17).

▲ The story of the Good Samaritan is found in the Gospel of Luke, chapter 10, verses 25 to 37 (Luke 10:25–37).

▶ The story of feeding five thousand people is found in four different places. One of these is in the Gospel of Mark, starting at chapter 6, verse 30 and ending at verse 44. (Mark 6:30–44)

Large chapter
number

In many ancient
manuscripts of the Bible
the texts were split into
sections to make it easier
to read. The chapter
sections in today's Bibles
were created by Stephen
Langton, who was
archbishop of Canterbury in
the thirteenth century. It
wasn't split into verses
until the sixteenth century.

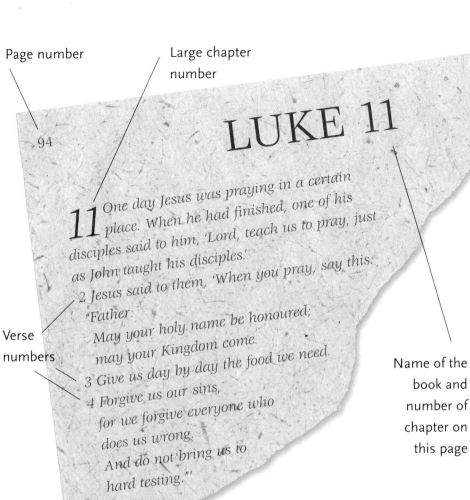

LUKE 11

94

11 One day Jesus was praying in a certain place. When he had finished, one of his disciples said to him, 'Lord, teach us to pray, just as John taught his disciples.'

2 Jesus said to them, 'When you pray, say this:

"Father:
May your holy name be honoured;
may your Kingdom come.

3 Give us day by day the food we need.

4 Forgive us our sins,
for we forgive everyone who
does us wrong.
And do not bring us to
hard testing."'

Verse
numbers

Name of the
book and
number of
chapter on
this page

THE BIBLE – NOT JUST A BOOK

In the past many people were unable to
read. For them to get to know the stories
of the Bible they had to listen to the
priest reading aloud to them. They
could also see the stories brought to life
for them through the windows of the
church. Many churches have stained
glass windows which show important
stories or events from the Bible.

▶This stained glass church window
shows an episode from the story of
Jonah when the sailors throw him
overboard and a big fish comes
and swallows him.

GOD LOVES EVERYONE

Throughout the Bible stories the writers show God's love for people. The writers of the New Testament believe that Jesus coming to earth was the most obvious sign of God's love. John's Gospel says this:

For God loved the world so much that he gave his only Son, so that everyone who believes in him may not die but have eternal life.

What is the Bible's message?

Christians believe that the Bible is a very important book; but what does it say to people today?

Many Christians read the Bible regularly, and they claim to learn new things from it all the time. Sometimes people read the Bible to find out what to do in a particular situation – to find out more about God and how God wants people to live.

Here are some important ideas found in the Bible:

LIVE IN PEACE

The Bible tells stories of people: they tell of God caring about how people treat one another, and wanting people to live peacefully and to treat one another fairly. This UN symbol is based on a quote from the Bible about peace:

The nations will hammer their swords into ploughs and their spears into pruning-knives.

LOOK AFTER THE WORLD

The Bible tells stories about the making of the world: they say it is God's world and people should care for it.

TELL OTHER PEOPLE

The books of the New Testament show how the first followers of Jesus went around telling everyone about Jesus and his teaching. Christians through the centuries have travelled the world passing on the news. John Wesley was famous in the eighteenth century for inspiring many ordinary people to become sincere Christians.

FORGIVE EACH OTHER

The Bible tells stories of people failing time and again to do the right thing. The prophets and Jesus talk of God's love and forgiveness. Jesus said that people should forgive each other as God forgives them. In Matthew's Gospel Jesus explains to Peter about forgiveness:

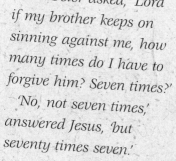

Then Peter asked, 'Lord if my brother keeps on sinning against me, how many times do I have to forgive him? Seven times?' 'No, not seven times,' answered Jesus, 'but seventy times seven.'

▲ John Wesley was a very popular preacher, whose whole life was devoted to following the Bible's message in a careful and methodical way.

LOVE EACH OTHER

The Bible tells about Jesus and his message that people should love God and one another, and be part of 'God's kingdom'. Jesus also talks of God's forgiveness, and speaks of God welcoming people as friends for ever.

GOD'S LOVE NEVER ENDS

The first Christians speak of how Jesus overcame death, and of their belief that death is not the end: because of their faith in Jesus, they believe they will be safe with God for ever.

Important Words

A

Angel a messenger from God.

Apocrypha a word that is sometimes used for the Deuterocanonical books.

Apostle any of Jesus' disciples sent to preach the Christian faith.

Aramaic one of the three languages in which the Bible was first written: a portion of Daniel was written in this language. Additionally, Jesus probably spoke Aramaic.

B

Baptism a ceremony when holy water is sprinkled on a person's head to symbolize their membership of the Christian church.

C

Canon the agreed list of books in the Bible.

Christ a title that means 'chosen king' or 'Messiah'. It comes from a Greek word.

Codex the word for a type of book that was used for writing from New Testament times.

Commandments special rules given to Moses by God.

Covenant an agreement. There were several between God and the people who became known as the Jews.

Crucifixion the way a person was put to death by being nailed to a wooden cross.

D

Dead Sea Scrolls ancient scrolls discovered in caves near the Dead Sea, which is in the southern part of the Bible lands. They had been hidden there for safety not long after the time of Jesus, by the Jewish religious community at nearby Qumran.

Deuterocanon a secondary list of books included in some Bibles but regarded by some scholars as of lesser importance.

Disciple one who learns from a teacher; a follower of Jesus.

Dictated words that have been dictated means that they were spoken by one person and written down by another.

E

Exile people who are in exile have been sent away from their native country.

G

Greek one of the three languages in which the Bible was first written. The New Testament was written in Greek.

H

Hebrew one of the three languages in which the Bible was first written. The Old Testament was written in Hebrew.

I

Israel the name of the people descended from Abraham, Isaac and Jacob (also called Israel). The people of Israel were also called Hebrews or, later, Jews.

J

Jerusalem the capital city in the land of the Jewish people. King David first made this city his capital.

Jews see 'Israel' above.

Judge a person chosen to decide on quarrels or disputes or matters relating to the Law.

M

Messiah a title that means 'chosen king' or 'Christ'. It comes from a Hebrew word.

O

Outcasts are people who have been rejected by their own people.

P

Papyrus a reed with dark green stems from which writing paper was made in ancient Egypt.

Parchment a fine leather specially prepared for writing on.

Pentateuch the first five books of the Old Testament.

Priest a priest was a person who helped people to understand God. Priests worked in the temples and organized acts of worship.

Prophet someone who received messages from God which were then passed on to the people. Some prophets could foretell the future.

Proverb a saying which has a deeper meaning.

Psalms psalms are sacred songs.

Q

Qumran the name of the monastery responsible for hiding scrolls in caves by the Dead Sea.

R

Resurrection the name given to Jesus' rising from the dead.

S

Scroll a document consisting of a long strip of writing material that can be rolled and unrolled to find the right place to read.

Septuagint an ancient Greek translation of the Old Testament.

Sinner someone who fails to live up to God's standard of goodness.

T

Temple a building for the worship of God. Solomon built the first temple in Jerusalem.

Testament an agreement or covenant.

Torah the first five books of the Old Testament.

V

Vellum a fine leather specially prepared for writing on.

Vision something seen in a dream or a trance.

Vulgate an ancient Latin translation of the Old Testament.

W

Worship to worship means to pray, praise and thank God.